THE BAT GUID[E]

GUID[E]

GOLF

Written by Sam Kotadia

Psychologist Sam Kotadia professionally helps top flight footballers stay focused and conquer the Bad Loser that lurks within us all. With this series of playful guides, Sam chucks his expertise out the window and offers strategies that are sure to lead to failure at every turn.

Illustrated by Nick Hilditch

Illustrator Nick Hilditch went off golf as a child when his Dad made him caddy for him in exchange for pocket money. So, in a way, his Bad Loser got the better of him before he'd ever taken a swing. His sport of choice is piercing inflated egos with the pointiest of pointy pencils. He teamed up with Sam to bring his skewed vision and irreverence to the Bad Loser's highly questionable advice.

Enjoy the game!

TO

....

FROM

....

Keep calm
on the first tee!

Winning is everything and you are fully aware that you need to put on a good show! To get ready for the all important first tee shot, make sure that you drink at least 10 espressos before you start. Getting the shakes, feeling your heartbeat in your head and the distant feeling of imminent danger is the sign of someone at his best.

Your self-respect, your dignity, and your self-worth is on the line. Fail to find the fairway on the 1st hole and your life will not be worth living!

Help your opponent when they lose their ball

You will try to win at all costs. If you find your oppositions ball before they do, STEP ON IT!

Striking the ball when it is slightly buried will give you a clear advantage.

They are to blame if they can't find their ball! Only idiots lose their balls, so you are completely justified by making life a little harder for them.

They will benefit from your tough love!

Don't blame
your clubs

You are the perfect golfer.

Not even Tiger Woods can compete with you when you are at the top of your game. The only rational explanation for playing a poor shot can only be down to your golf-clubs malfunctioning. The only solution is to dispose of them!

If you run out of clubs on the course go and drown your sorrows in the clubhouse.

Remember you can always buy new clubs when your Nike sponsorship fee arrives at the end of the month.

Hold your nerve
on short putts

Short putts don't scare you.

You are fully aware golf matches are won and lost on the green.

You can make any short putt with your eyes closed.

You've published several books on Mastering The Short Game, so there is no need to get nervous on the green.

You have never missed a short putt in your life. All of that practise in your living-room has clearly paid off.

Don't blame
the weather

The weather doesn't bother you.

Severe weather conditions such as
gales, floods, persistent snow, and
torrential rain fail to
damage your game;
in fact they
improve it.

They make you focus and they sharpen you up!

Some of your best rounds have come from having to strike the ball backwards due to heavy winds and having to make routine putts underwater.

Keep your calm
with slow players

Coming up against slow players is more painful than death.

When you encounter them it feels like you will explode. Make sure you tell them exactly what you think of them!!! If they don't speed up, start firing golf balls in their direction.

There is no need to ask for permission to play through when you encounter slow play. Don't even acknowledge the other players as you stroll by.

Win graciously

"Winning isn't everything" is a phrase coined by life's unfortunates.

Of course winning is everything; you play to win and nothing else. If you can't savour your victories with the most outrageous celebrations... what's the point? Fist punching the air and screaming "get in!!!" is yesterday's news.

Focus on celebrations that are truly outrageous.

Savour your success for as long as possible in the face of life's second best. It might help them to buck up their ideas for next time!

Respect the wildlife

The wildlife are pests out on the golf course.

Suggest to the greenkeeper to lay down the most brutal of traps to keep them at bay. Golf courses are no place for creatures much further down the food chain.

You are at the top of the food chain, giving you the right to exterminate any critters that distract you from your game. There is no harm in carrying a rifle with you. Besides, zoning in on the wildlife will give you something to do whilst your opponents are taking their shot.

Respect the dress code

No one tells you what to wear when you are out on the golf course.

Someone with your talent raises the profile of your golf club irrespective of what you are wearing.

To ensure that your golf club
doesn't take you for granted keep a
selection of outrageous outfits in
the back of your car.

Reserve the most outrageous
ones only for the most prestigious
golfing occasions.

Always shake hands

There is no need to be polite after a round of golf; win or lose.

It is a privilege for your opponents to have the opportunity to play alongside one of the greats.

Snub any gesture to shake hands with utter contempt.

Shaking hands is for wimps. It is war on the golf course and being a good sport doesn't exist when the golf clubs are out!

The Bad Losers Guides ™

Published by Mindsport Ltd in 2012- All rights reserved. Printed in China